The Lonely Christmas Tre

Written By Lila-Ann Gray

Illustrated By Jean Darling

© Lila-Ann Gray 2021

To Eldon

love
Lila-Ann +

Terms and Conditions

LEGAL NOTICE

Published by Babysteps Publishing Limited All enquires to kevin@babystepspublishing.com

ISBN-13 9798485393212

The Lonely Christmas Tree

It was a beautiful spring day, and the woods were slowly waking up after a long hard winter.

The sun was shining, and its beams of light felt warming to the trees. There were new buds growing everywhere, and a feeling of great excitement seemed to weave in and out of the whole woodland.

Little animals that had slept their way through the winter were waking up and peeking out of their cosy homes to feel the wonderful sunlight on their small furry bodies.

As a gentle breeze rustled through the new leaves growing on the trees, the trees themselves were talking happily to each other. One voice could be heard above the others. It was the old oak tree who stood in the middle of the wood, his booming voice grumbling as usual about something.

"What's old grumpy pants moaning about today?" they asked each other. Then his loud complaining voice called out, "what is this thing growing here next to me, far too close to my tree trunk. The very nerve of it. Wake up and tell us who you are this minute."

The little tree woke up at the sound of such a complaining voice and was very frightened at what the old oak tree was saying to him. "When you were asleep at the beginning of the year, my human family brought me here and planted me in this spot." At that, he started to cry, and there was a murmuring of sympathy among the other trees, all listening intently to the little Christmas tree's story.

"They had bought me as their Christmas tree," he continued, trying hard to stop crying. "It was wonderful. They dressed me up in tinsel and hung shiny, pretty baubles from my branches. They put some sparkly lights all through them that flashed on and off. They made such a fuss of me, and I was so happy. On the very top of my tree, they placed a beautiful fairy doll, who came alive at night, and we would laugh and sing together. I miss her and my human family so much, and I have been so terribly lonely." With that, he cried even louder.

The old oak tree felt ashamed that he had been so grumpy and apologised to the little tree. "There, there, young fella, don't take on so, I didn't realise how unhappy you were or how lonely, and I am so sorry for being so sharp," he said in a quiet and gentle voice that was unusual for him. "We will look after you. You're still very small and young. I am sure you will grow big and strong; we will all be your friends and watch over you."

"Oh, thank you so much," replied the little Christmas tree, already feeling much happier. "I would love to have some friends to talk to, and I am sure it will help me to not feel so lonely because I can't help missing my human family."

As spring turned into summer, the trees grew more beautiful by the day, and the woods buzzed with activity. Squirrels ran up and down tree trunks, bouncing up and down on branches and chattering animatedly to each other, making a lot of noise. Badgers roamed around at night while their babies ran in and out of their underground homes.

Rabbits hopped around whilst birds sang from high branches, butterflies weaved in and out of flowers, and bees buzzed around in their search for pollen. Life was indeed very busy in the woods, and it became a magical place to the little

Christmas tree as he watched with joy all the activity around him. But he still missed his human family and his friend, the fairy.

The birds, animals, and insects noticed that as hard as he tried to keep cheerful, the little Christmas tree seemed a little sad at times, and so everyone did their best to make him feel happy and loved.

Occasionally a couple of passing deer would come exploring the woods, and they were very happy to stop for a chat with the trees and the animals. They were rather scared of any noises and didn't like the way the leaves sometimes rustled at their feet if there was a breeze and the squirrel children loved going boo on them, so they were always rather on edge and ready to run and hide

One day the little Christmas tree, which appeared to be growing much bigger now, felt a tickling sensation on his tree trunk and a loud drilling noise filled his senses. "What's happening to me?" he shouted worriedly. The other trees reassured him that all was well. They explained he had no need to worry as it was only Percy, the woodpecker.

"Oh dear," said Percy. "I am so sorry for scaring you. You obviously haven't been visited by woodpeckers before. We love a bit of softwood occasionally. I was passing through the woods today on my way home, and I thought you looked very inviting. I normally  prefer the bark of the larger trees, but the sun was shining on you, and you looked rather delicious."

A squirrel family would often visit the little Christmas tree, and the two baby squirrels would tickle his pine needles as they raced each other up and down his branches. He loved to hear their laughter and chatter. They would enjoy getting into mischief. Their favourite pastime was for one of them to hang upside down on a branch while the other one tried to tickle their paws to make them fall off. This would bring squeals of laughter from them both.

Mummy squirrel would end up very hot and bothered and very cross, apologising profusely for the bad behaviour of her little children.

As always, after summer came autumn, and things started to quieten down in the woods. Many of the trees lost their leaves. Flowers were no longer blossoming. The bees no longer buzzed around looking for pollen to make their honey. The butterflies had disappeared into their warm cocoons. The squirrel family didn't visit as often as they were very busy collecting nuts and other food to store away to see them through the winter.

The nights became darker earlier, and there was a quietening down of everything, rather like tucking down cosily in bed ready to fall asleep.

The little Christmas tree started to feel more and more lonely. Nobody came to visit anymore. The old oak tree next to him was feeling his age and fell asleep long before the others, not even bothering to stir when the wind blew hard, and his leaves silently fell to the ground. There were storms with loud booms of thunder, lightning striking fear into some of the trees in case it

pierced their trunks and gave them burns. When it rained and did not stop for days, the raindrops would settle on their branches and tickle them with every drop that fell to the ground—no wonder the trees just wanted to sleep instead of constantly feeling cold and miserable.

The lonely little Christmas tree often cried himself to sleep. He did not realise how big and beautiful he had become during the months he had been in the woods

Then as winter took hold over all the woodland, everything became still and quiet. Nothing stirred. The little Christmas tree wondered how he would get through the next few months until spring came back, and the woods would come to life again. He thought with such longing of the last Christmas when he was with his human family. He knew it was nearly Christmas time now, and he started to cry as he missed them and the fairy doll so much.

With those sad thoughts uppermost in his mind, he tried to quieten down, and as he closed his eyes, it was with a heavy heart that he finally managed to fall asleep.

He was woken up with a start; there was a strange noise coming from the bottom of his trunk. He felt a moment of fear as the deep darkness of the woods engulfed him. He could just see the snow was falling; no wonder he was feeling rather chilly as well as scared. Then a lantern moved its light

towards someone digging him out of the ground, and he could see the figure of a man and two little children warmly clad, one holding the lantern while the other jumped up and down in excitement. It was his human family. They had come back for him.

Daddy finished digging and laid him gently on the ground. Paul and Sally, the two children who he loved so much, helped daddy carry him carefully home, which fortunately wasn't that far from the woods

When they arrived at the house, mummy stood on the front step holding tight to the family's new baby. "Oh, our beautiful little Christmas tree, we have missed you so much." she said "daddy was right. By leaving you in the woods in the shelter of some other trees, he said you would grow strong and tall until we could fetch you home again for Christmas and just look at you now. You look wonderful". Paul and Sally help to get him in and settled, and we can all

decorate him, and then you can both place the fairy doll at the top where she loves to sit.

The children enjoyed a very happy hour with mummy and daddy putting all the beautiful decorations back on the Christmas tree once more. The tinsel was all the colours of the rainbow, the baubles sparkled, and the lights twinkled merrily on and off in green, red, and blue.

Mummy and daddy were holding the baby whose little hands kept coming out to grab a bauble; Paul and Sally stepped back to admire their darling not so little Christmas tree. "After this Christmas," mummy said," We will take you back to your home in the woods so that you can rest until next Christmas when we will collect you again. We cannot imagine Christmas without you now."

The not so little Christmas tree felt even taller and stronger, happier than he had ever been. Not only was he to be with his human family every Christmas, he would rejoin his wonderful friends in the woods, and he need never feel like he was a lonely Christmas tree ever again.

About the Author

Born in Cornwall, I was the only daughter of aging parents with two much older brothers, who travelled to exotic places with the Royal Navy and returning home bearing gifts for their little sister, who would then make up

tales of far away adventures.

As a young adult, I had various jobs ranging from police cadet to dental nursing, but I especially loved my time as a teaching assistant at a local primary school, which gave me the freedom to story tell.

I live in a little village in West Sussex nestled between the South Downs and the sea, so I have plenty of scope for my imagination to work on.

My storytelling journey really began with my father making up the adventures of two little rabbits. I then started telling my own children stories. In fact, my daughter refused to have her hair washed without a favourite tale. I carried on the tradition with my grandchildren, and now I am blessed with two beautiful great-granddaughters who have been my inspiration for my series of books, 'The Magical Adventures with Granny.' My eldest great-granddaughter is three years old, and she has reignited my passion for magic and the power of the imagination. When she and I are together, we live in a world of trees that hide the fairy folk, animals, and birds who talk to us along

with big sprinkles of sparkly fairy dust and we find ourselves drawn into exciting made-up adventures.
I like to think my books will encourage children to use their imaginations as a tool to believe in themselves.

You can visit Lila's Facebook page for more fantastic information at:

https://www.facebook.com/Granny-Lilas-Childrens-books-207876791276149/

or on Instagram: grannylilaschildrensbooks

One More Thing Before You Go…

If you enjoyed reading this book or found it useful, I'd be very grateful if you'd post a short review on Amazon. Your support really does make a difference, and I read all the reviews personally, so I can get your feedback and make this and future books even better.

If you would like to leave a review, then all you need to do is click the review link on Amazon here:

https://amzn.to/3lfcPrh

 Thanks again for your support!

Printed in Great Britain
by Amazon